Leadership, Vision and Reality

Keisha Lanell Merchant

Tribute: To the Future and The

Egalitarian World

To My Family, Love Ones, Environment and Community, My Beloved World: Be Safe and Revolutionize the Internal Self, Stay Unified and be Whole

Leadership, Vision and Reality

The leader is not just born and trained into a leader, but it is a construct as well. The leader and the role of a leader consist of: the vision, the action plan and the teams that provide the support, access, resources, and the production to build a vision from the stages of human development blueprints into the creation of the reality of the leader's vision. Northouse, (2016) discusses the traits, skills, and theories of the leadership role and the leader. The structures of identities that are considered as constructivism theory and trait, skills and style approach of the leader can be seen as the illustration of a cake with important ingredients. The process of making a leader, and the process of forming an administration team, and finally the followership of a leader depends on the style of a leader.

The Construction of the Leader and the Leadership Role

Northouse, (2016), examines the personality of a leader. The evaluation and assessment of leadership can be examine through tests as the Myers and Briggs Type Indicator or Eyesnck Personality Questionnaire. Other evaluations as the Cultural Schema Theory, (1999), can also be determine by an external observation, monitoring system for patterns, configurations and conformation traits that can be used to categorize external factors of a personality and its temperaments.

Perceptions are another key factors of construction in leadership, Ismail, Mohamad, Mohamed, Rafiuddin, and Zhen, (2010).discusses the transformative and transactional leadership roles as a perception assessment in design. Ismail et al. (2010), concludes that perception can influence surveys and interviews, and alter the outcome and results of a sample or study. The leadership model cannot be identified as an accurate design since leadership is a model of perception or construct of perception. Perception is the leading roles in leadership. Perception and trust becomes the characteristic in leadership. The study of leadership can identify with the construct of perception, and the model of trait approach, skill approach and style approach as to psychodynamic approach can lead to the very necessary elements of perception, trust and the characteristics of opinions. The aspect of judgment can be construed to be a strong factor due to the background history and knowledge base of a leader. The totality of the temperament of a leader rest on influences of the environment whether external and internal cognizance.

The Forming of Teams and Leaders

Management and Leaders have this in difference that is the followership and the delegation or regulation of a task, vision, and journey as a motivation. Kotter, (2001) discusses the motivation of a leader and the manager. The motivation of a leader is different in many ways. The leader's motivation is different through these three dynamics: vision setting versus planning and staffing versus supporting. The vision setting involve in a followership and a strong leading that teams are motivated to be content in the environment whether it is a work place, in the field or under the process of policies, protocols and procedures. These practices are the theoretical framework that the teams are able to follow in line with the ambiance of the environment which carries and embodies the vision of the leader.

Strang and Kuhnert (2009) mentions the constructive development theory that also motivates leaders and managers to evaluate development through constructive identification. This psychological development can be the access to the motivation framework that teams and leaders structure their management as to administer change

and implement motivation as to high or

low performance teams. The cognitive

development of perception can be a

theoretical framework to initiate and

create policies around similar

assessments, evaluation and

examinations to assist in the process of

managing or leading teams through

realization of the development of

behavior, as to cognitive perception,

emotional and socio economical

perception and other areas of interest

that develops reality through the lens of

perception in the forming of teams to perform and achieve goals.

Motivation can be an underlying factor to leaders and managers in formulating a team, and organizing a team to achieve a task, activity and mission. Vroom and Jago (2007), focuses on the contingent theory as another theory used to build a theoretical framework for leaders to produce motivation to accomplish through a crisis or situation and not bail out or retreat from opposition or conflict, complicated as to complex situations that can deviation or undo a goal. The adaptive principle to associate leaders with their followers to perform under pressure without the loss of motivation and morale. In any case, leaders are constructed identities to target teams to move progress under circumstances external or internal tendencies that may distract anyone from the common ground and common goal to complete in a given situation. The leader-member relationship is very important in building a vision in a company. The challenges required adaptability in order for the leader to build structures using the contingency theory to construct policies, procedures, processes and practices to assemble and the production to perform a task under extreme tests, trials and prosecutions.

Motivation and Power

Avolio, Walumbwa and Weber (2009) approach to motivation and power is through the leadership theory and theoretical framework of the future forecast as a predicator of change. The authentic and complexity leadership focuses on change as a primary key factor to motivate teams to drive to their best performance. High performing teams are effective through change and managing change. The ability to adapt to change, can decrease conflict, regulate disparities and to delegate sustainability and satisfaction evenly. The authentic leadership model construct an identity that identifies with the needs of the team's first source. Honest relationship, ethical foundation and encourages equal support for all teams and their environment to be open and blended. The complexity leadership role model construct an identity that identifies with the traditions of completing a task first before reward or incentives. The servant leadership carries the task as a primary goal over the needs of a leader and the teams to achieve deadlines and mastery of progress over satisfaction. The traditional role that a task is more important or the goal is more important in the journey over the motivation to be satisfied in the process. The satisfaction of a role in a task is secondary rather primary. The models are constructs of motivation and power fundamentally collections in the task and situation of decision making when a leader must lead and regulate change through adapting to the teams needs to motivate them or the social power to drive a production of the

team to finish a task's deadline in a
timely manner and then target the needs
of the team.

Critical examination that social
power can be an excuse to ignore the
needs of the teams in the leader's
process to handle a goal in a timely
manner in "fear" of competitive
disadvantages, costs, risks, liabilities and
burdens that can deplete resources
quickly and decrease productivity and the
return of investment to the stakeholders
that are interested in the investment of a
task and not so much the teams. The
critical strategy is to find a leadership

15

model as to transformative leadership that have adaptive abilities to use the social power and motivation to equally satisfy and structure needs and goals to empower and resolve any complications in the process of meeting the deadlines and external and internal values, ethics or principles of a leader and their journey with their teams or subordinates as to resistance and difficult or low performers.

Developing Teams and Leaders

George, Sims, McLean and Mayer, (2007) discusses the theoretical framework of social power and motivation through the authentic leadership framework. The process of developing a team. The self-awareness factors are asking leaders and teams to target on self-autonomy. The framework is to use responsibility, creativity and self-examination of weaknesses and strengths. The values of a leader and their teams as individuals and as a group can be identified as their ethics through self-monitoring, consistency and resiliency. The process of authentic leadership construct can be identified also the progress of communication system through the use of their motivation and social power to control or influence their environment and teams and overcome resistance and difficulty or low performers.

George, et al. (2007), also portrays the authentic leadership as a equal match with the transformative leadership construct as to the ability to implement change as to creativity, innovation, invention and the expansion methods of competitive advantage using development as a tool to produce ethics and resilience rather exploitation, abuse, neglect and discount. The authentic process to self-monitor, self-evaluate and self-govern through daily operating services to use resources, equality, ethics and trust to facilitate change, increase mobility, innovation and integrity by solidifying commitment, engagement and trusting relationships, the authentic leadership model and transformative leadership model use change to influence their teams to drive their motivation and social power to promote optimism and trustworthiness through a collective cognizance approach of growth and egalitarianism in morale.

Conflict in Power

Maner and Mead (2010), discusses the tension between leaders

usage of power and the recipients of
tension. The self-serving leaders
construct disables the potential
productivity of teams through the break
down factors of: perspective, power and
decision making that leads to pressure,
strain, stress and trauma. The injury of
damage, grievance, hardship and harm,
can become part of the environment and
energy in the external and internal
factors of the construction of the self-
serving leader. Self-serving leaders can
become aggressively bias that depletes
resources quickly, increase long term
risks, liabilities and burdens that can

cause detrimental and permanent
damages and costs to the longevity and
life cycle of a company, their teams, and
complicate their results in the process
also increase conflicts and urgent
situations that lead into struggles, wars,
battles, clashes and division as to
separation, detachment and disparities or
inconsistencies. Posner (2010),
discusses the impacts of congruency as
follows can be seen as stated above in
the conflicts of self-serving leadership
modeling and power misused through
such elements of bias, partiality,
preferentialism, preference, subjectivity

and one-sidedness to delegate and regulate influence with teams and subordinates (resistance).

The impact of congruency can be also identified in the appropriateness as stated that authentic leadership models are contrasted to the self-serving leadership model through the ability to come together and the lack thereof. The components that connect and collect teams and leaders through certain type of traits, skills, values, perceptions, perspectives, style and ethics can associate people to be motivated or to be disengaged and resist through injury or conflict. Raven (1993) discusses the practice of social concerns through the process of thought as to French and Raven's pivotal research on power (as to supremacy, control, command, rule and influence) surveyed the six ranks of power: reward, coercion, legitimate, expert, referent, and informational.

The disconnect blocks of barriers, obstacles and obstructions to justice through the lack of congruency can decrease morale and increase conflict, resistance and injuries in a working environment, and also at whole with the totality of costs, burden, liabilities and increase of risks that eliminate the certainty of return of investment, bottom line and productivity that can increase green practices, ethical distribution and egalitarian modifications. These impacts have an effect on change, development, growth, advancement and expansion.

Ethical Leadership

Northouse (2016), discusses ethical leadership as defined as responsibility or the intentions to be responsible in behavior, attitude and cognition processes to build teams and decrease resistance through trust and increase appropriateness for each individual. The ethical leadership can be weighed equally with the transformative leadership model and the authentic leadership model. The formula to be responsible for the team as a whole network system and stakeholder system to work together through connection, trust and satisfaction as a performance base model to increase the art and presentation of a vision through the application process of certainty and commitment. The values and perception is to increase the response time to meet the needs of the teams in resources, equipment, environment as to ambiance, including the interaction with the

environment as an external factor of

wellness and internal factors as to

psychological health care and quality

standards to provide teams to develop

their own personal goals and group goals

to initiate innovation, as to change,

invention and advancement using the

tools of modernization, improvement and

upgrading systems to be adaptive. The

adjustments and flexibility to observe,

monitor and be engaged with the process

of responsibility and the bond of

collectiveness, inclusivity and cultural

conscientious.

The matriculation of bridging the gaps with diversification and articulation of social and artistic values that promote principles, beliefs philosophies to be ethical. The results of ethical leaders can be the productivity and outcome of decrease in stressful working environment and the increase in satisfaction of group collectiveness. Abrhiem (2012) clarifies that differences between personal ethics and group or cultural ethics as to the spectrum and continuums of ethical behavior in groups and self-actualization processes. The deontological and teleological ethical theories can carry some opponent views that divide groups, teams, and individuals. Teleological ethical theories can be developed through a bias notion of self-serving perceptions of what ethics entail. Deontological duties to insist leaders to value others as an obligation to their journey. The limitations and expectations of ethics with the individual and in a group as to the working environment or ambiance of the entirety of the results of the arrangements of the vision and the needs of the teams.

Bagozzi, Sekerka and Hill (2009) virtues of ethics that can be a collective

cultural values to be developed as

consequentialism, (to eliminate harm)

and emotionalism (to increase support)

and empiricism (to increase traditions).

Cuilla (2011), discusses the historical

and modern outcomes of ethics in

general. Resulting the critical component

of change, improvement and

development of human societies and

cultural impacts that diversified the

strengths of the human psyche and

decrease injury of communities. The

modern world and work load is based on

empiricism model of ethics that is the

poor standards of traditions that are on

the values of self-serving leadership models that cater to favoritism and partiality in the socialization structures and systems. The future models may lead to consequentialism to eliminate harm and the emotionalism to increase support for understanding the values of experiences of individuals and groups to companion change, improvement and maturity. The employee and CEO unifies in the sense that ethical behavior increases compensation as an egalitarian system and the support system to construct the duality of networking and communications to be collective in lowering costs, risks,

burdens and liabilities through trust,

equality and responsibility.

Conclusion

Innovation, Revolutionary and

Ground-Breaking

Nothouse (2016), discusses, Hill's

leadership model as the ability to be

effective with teams. The effective notion

is to be active and committed to engage

and participate with the personal and
group goals as to self-awareness and
group awareness model to develop and
grow without the micromanagement
system of self-serving bias and self-
serving leadership constructs of self-
interest to profit and exploit the use of
progress and confiscate resources to
neglect others, abusive power and ignore
needs to build a vision in a timely manner
under rigid and strict deadlines, values
and principles that dominate others
through control, coercing and partiality
systematic methods, traditions that lead
to dysfunction, work stress and injuries

(damages and high costs, risks and burden, liabilities).

Innovation can be a tool and construct that identifies the modern world and the change from the ancient world that demonstrates evidence of elevation and rise of cultural and societal development as a social notion to a collaboration and collective of ideas that promote positive change and optimal improvement. The vision of a leader involve the building blocks of: development, examination, awareness and trust to attract collectiveness, inclusivity and unification among groups

33

and individuals working toward a goal, task, overcoming a situation within a vision or mission to be fully understood through the accuracy and diversification of revolutionary creativity.   Ayman and Korabik (2010), discusses the impact of social binaries and social roles as to gender and culture stereotypes. The negative effects of obstructions to therapeutically promoted policies that can allow all groups to be in an egalitarian network system to collaborate and be collective for a vision to work for a purpose, task and goal as to eliminate injury, harm and damage of environment and humanity through collective innovation and community building to construct and identify teams and leaders in a team leadership role for building and not destroying morale to maturity.

Revolutions are resistances that lead to revolutionary and ground breaking achievements that propels a society at large into the increase prospective of advancements and expansions. Balthazard, Waldman and Warren (2009) discusses the innovations of virtual and technologies that increase certainty and revolutionizes the authentication of transformation,

35

communication systems and collectiveness. The promises of revolutions that consist of revolts, resistances, civil disobediences and negative impacts of uprising and mutiny can be another means to change. The itinerary to change can be done in an effective way or an ineffective approach to revolutionary production and transformation to improvement. The differences between revolutions and revolutionary progress is the type of leadership that is responsible for the future.

Eagly and Lau Chin (2010) discusses diversity and equality. The notion to egalitarian models in the work place and in the civility of the environment. Revolutions have been an ancient practice to remind self-serving leaders that teams are unsatisfied, and their needs are being ignored. Their time and trust are being exploited. The model of leadership can be examined through the social issues of current and past artifacts that show patterns of behavior, conflict and examine the theories and approaches of leaders ability to innovate, revolutionize and build ground breaking achievements to satisfy their teams, environment, communities to socialize collectively for the purpose of a goal, task and vision to implement for their promotion and welfare to elevate and rise. Teams are interested in the integration to increase in holistic values as to compensation, quality care, safety, reasonable responsibility and not feel obligated to be damaged to the workloads that decrease their health, wellness, welfare and quality lifestyles to be satisfied, fulfilled and rewarded as a collective conscious that is conscientious and matured through the thorough

LEADERSHIP, VISION AND REALITY

collaboration that becomes the essence

of improvement and mastery of self and

group autonomy through team leadership

models that function visions using the

approach of authentication, ethics and

transformation. The future is in the hands

of the leadership and team(s) that can be

high performers through communication,

commitment, collectiveness, egalitarian

networking and trust bonds that promote

improvement, innovation and excellence

in morale, quality living and equality

distribution in resources, access to

growth and maturity, and repairing of

mistakes that is effective team

leadership.

References

Abrhiem, T. H. (2012). Ethical leadership: Keeping values in business culture. *Business & Management Review, 2*(7), 11–19. Retrieved from https://www.waldenu.edu

Avolio, B. J., Walumbwa, F. O., & Weber, T. J. (2009). Leadership: Current theories, research, and future directions. *Annual Review of Psychology, 60*(1), 421–449. Retrieved from https://www.waldenu.edu

Ayman, R., & Korabik, K. (2010). Leadership: Why gender and culture matter. American Psychologist, 65(3), 157–170. Retrieved from https://www.waldenu.edu

Bagozzi, R., Sekerka, L., & Hill, V. (2009). Hierarchical motive structures and their role in moral choices. *Journal of Business Ethics, 90,* 461–486. Retrieved from https://www.waldenu.edu

Balthazard, P. A., Waldman, D. A., & Warren, J. E. (2009). Predictors of the emergence of transformational leadership in virtual decision teams. Leadership Quarterly, 20(5), 651–663. Retrieved from https://www.waldenu.edu

Cuilla, J. B. (2011). Is business ethics getting better? A historical perspective. *Business Ethics Quarterly, 21*(2), 335–343. Retrieved from https://www.waldenu.edu

Eagly, A. H., & Lau Chin, J. (2010). Diversity and leadership in a changing world. American Psychologist, 65(3), 216–224. Retrieved from https://www/waldenu.edu

George, B., Sims, P., McLean, A. N., & Mayer, D. (2007). Discovering your authentic leadership.*Harvard Business Review, 85*(2), 129–138. Retrieved from the http://www.waldenu.edu

Ismail, A., Mohamad, M. H., Mohamed, H. A.-B., Rafiuddin, N. M., & Zhen, K. W. P. (2010). Transformational and transactional leadership styles as a predictor of individual outcomes. *Theoretical & Applied Economics*, *17*(6), 89–104. Retrieved from https://www.waldenu.edu

Kotter, J. P. (2001). What leaders really do. *Harvard Business Review*, *79*(11), 85–96. Retrieved from the https://www.waldenu.edu

Maner, J. K., & Mead, N. L. (2010). The essential tension between leadership and power: When leaders sacrifice group goals for the sake of self-interest. *Journal of Personality and Social Psychology*, *99*(3), 482–497.

Northouse, P. G. (2016). *Leadership: Theory and practice* (7th ed.). Thousand Oaks, CA: Sage.

Posner, B. (2010). Another look at the impact of personal and organizational values congruency. *Journal of Business Ethics, 97*(4), 535–541. Retrieved from https://www.waldenu.edu.

Raven, B. H. (1993). The bases of power: Origins and recent developments. *Journal of Social Issues, 49*(4), 227–251. Retrieved from https://www.waldenu.edu

Strang, S. E., & Kuhnert, K. W. (2009). Personality and leadership developmental levels as predictors of leader performance.*Leadership Quarterly, 20*(3), 421–433. Retrieved from https://www.waldenu.edu

Vroom, V. H., & Jago, A. G. (2007). The role of the situation in leadership. *American Psychologist,62*(1), 17–24. Retrieved from https://www.waldenu.edu